TUNING THE PEDAL STEEL

TUNING TO THE PIANO

Basic Open Tuning

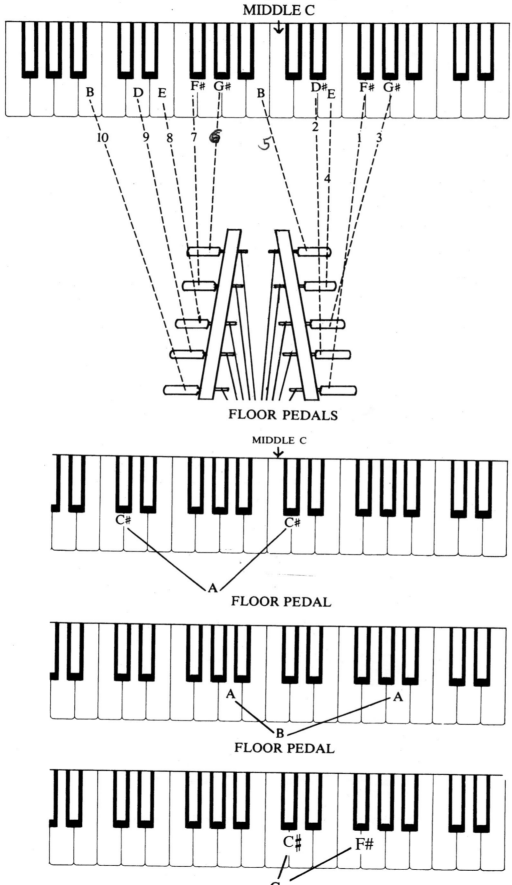

MIDDLE C

FLOOR PEDALS

MIDDLE C

FLOOR PEDAL

FLOOR PEDAL

PEDAL STEEL GUITAR TUNING CHART

FLOOR PEDALS USED

	A	B	C	STRINGS	GAUGES
F#				1	013
D#				2	015
G#		A		3	011
E			F#	4	014
B	C#		C#	5	017
G#		A		6	020
F#				7	026W
E				8	030W
D				9	034W
B	C#			10	036W

Hertz(HZ) Tuning Numbers
(not Cents)

E9th Tuning
(Electronic Tuner)

THE PEDALS ___(A) ___ (B) ___ (C)

(1)F#(441.5)
(2)D#(439)
(3)G#(439) _____ A(441)
(4)E(442.5) _____ F#(439.5)
(5)B(442) _____ C#(438.5) ___ C#(438.5)
(6)G#(439) _____ A(441)
(7)F#(441.5)
(8)E(442.5)
(9)D(441.5)
(10)B(442) ____ C#(438.5)

TABLATURE INSTRUCTION
(Knowledge of Music Not Required)
Strings and Frets

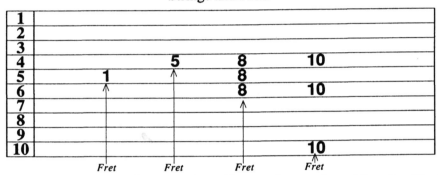

The spaces are numbered downward one through ten. These are the ten strings of the guitar. The numbers positioned in the spaces are the frets on which you are to place the bar. The three eights (strings 4-5-6) and the three tens (strings 4-6-10) are to be played all three at the same time (chord) using the thumb, first, and second fingers.

TIMING

NOTES

WHOLE 4 COUNTS	HALF 2 COUNTS	QUARTER 1 COUNT	EIGHTH 2 FOR 1 COUNT

RESTS

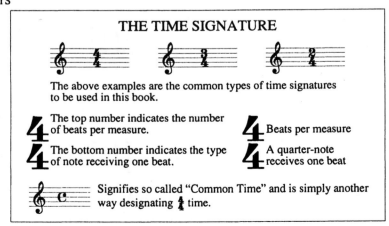

THE TIME SIGNATURE

The above examples are the common types of time signatures to be used in this book.

4 The top number indicates the number of beats per measure.
4 The bottom number indicates the type of note receiving one beat.

4 Beats per measure
4 A quarter-note receives one beat

C Signifies so called "Common Time" and is simply another way designating 4/4 time.

MEL BAY'S EASIEST COUNTRY PEDAL STEEL GUITAR BOOK

By Dewitt Scott

© 1994 BY MEL BAY PUBLICATIONS, INC., PACIFIC, MO 63069.
ALL RIGHTS RESERVED. INTERNATIONAL COPYRIGHT SECURED. B.M.I. MADE AND PRINTED IN U.S.A.

Visit us on the Web at http://www.melbay.com — E-mail us at email@melbay.com

CONTENTS

EXPLANATION OF SIGNS AND SYMBOLS

    A pedal is depressed (Raise strings 5 and 10).

    B pedal is depressed (Raise strings 3 and 6).

B   Depress both pedals together.

C   Pedals raise strings 3 and 6 (G♯'s to A) and raise strings 4 (E to F♯) and 5 (B to C♯).

    Single numbers receive 1 count.

7   Numbers connected by an arc are eighth notes.

7   Dotted quarter tied to eighth note.

    Gliss sign-Pick the first note and slide to the second note. Ex. 6 7. DO NOT pick the 7. SLIDE into it.

    Sustain for the duration of the sign.

9   Slide into the 9. Could vary from 1/2 to 1 fret.

GLISS OR SLIDES

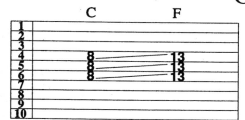

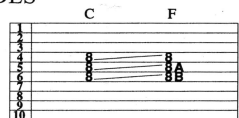

Gliss = Slide from lower notes to the higher notes without picking the higher notes.

Gliss Effect With Pedals = Pick the strings without pedals, while the strings are still ringing push the A and B pedals down.

Some Hints on Pick Blocking

The tune "Two String Melody" is an excellent choice for your first solo as the entire tune is played on two strings only. This allows you to limit your concentration to just two strings and it is also an excellent opportunity to learn pick blocking.

HOW TO PICK BLOCK

Step #1. The bar remains on the strings and is moved very quickly from one fret to another.

Step #2. Pick strings 5 and 6 at the 3rd fret on the melody "Two String Melody." (Page 6)

Step #3. Pick the same two strings again with the same two fingers and move the bar very quickly to the 8th fret and pick the same two strings again. It is a very fast movement. ALSO, place your picks on the strings just BEFORE you move the bar. You will eliminate the beautiful slide that the steel guitar is known for but it is your first step in learning to pick block.

WHICH PICKS SHOULD YOU USE?

As there is no set rule for this you must experiment and find the method that will work best for you. Examples:

    A. 1st and 2nd fingers.

    B. Thumb and 1st finger.

    C. Thumb and 2nd finger.

    D. A combination of all three.

(Page 7 uses the same rule—you will find thumb and second finger work the best)

GLISS OR SLIDES

Gliss = Slide from lower note to the higher note without picking the higher note.

1	
2	
3	
4	8 ———— 13
5	8 ———— 13
6	8 ———— 13
7	
8	
9	
10	

Gliss = Slide from the higher note to the lower note without picking the lower note.

1	
2	
3	
4	13 ———— 8
5	13 ———— 8
6	13 ———— 8
7	
8	
9	
10	

Gliss Effect With Pedals = Pick the strings without pedals, while the strings are still ringing push the A and B pedals down.

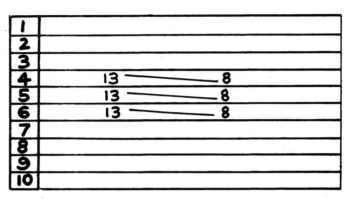

1	
2	
3	
4	8 ———— 8
5	8 ———— 8A
6	8 ———— 8B
7	
8	
9	
10	

Gliss Effect With Pedals = Pick the strings with the A and B pedals down. While the strings are still ringing release the A and B pedals.

1	
2	
3	
4	8 ———— 8
5	8A ———— 8
6	8B ———— 8
7	
8	
9	
10	

Sustain = ～～～～～～
Sound is carried over and not picked again but is counted.

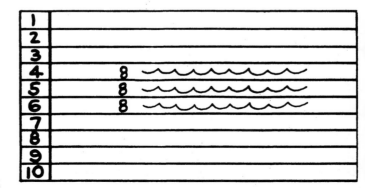

6

RIGHT AND LEFT HAND POSITIONS

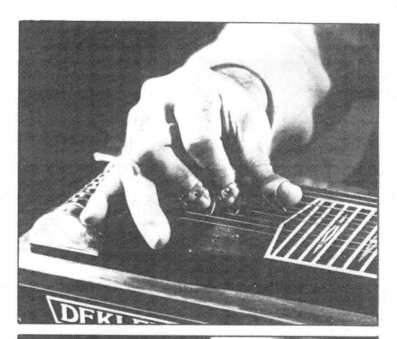

Right Hand

Ring and little fingers are extended out with side of palm blocking the strings.

Right Hand

Ring and little fingers are tucked under with the fingers blocking the treble strings and the palm blocking the bass strings.

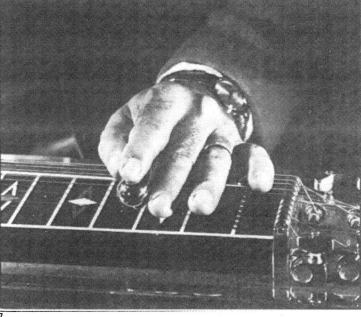

Left Hand

The ring and little finger rest on the strings.

Two String Melody

By DeWitt Scott

(Use Thumb and Second Finger)

The Old Rugged Cross

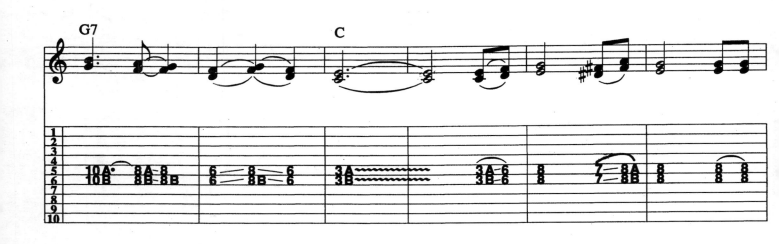

Steel Guitar Boogie

By DeWitt Scott

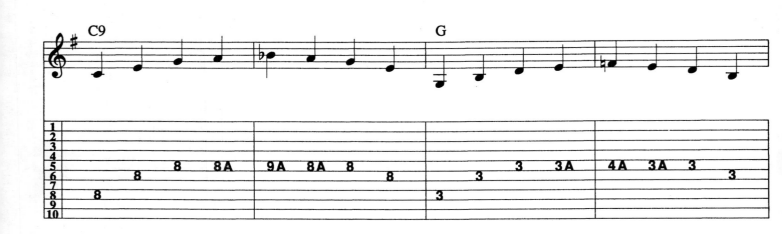

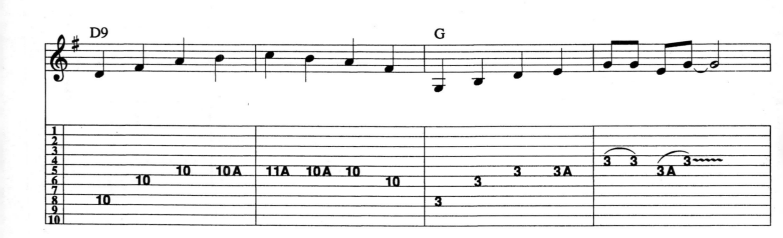

Ad lib solo-Keep the A pedal depressed throughout the entire solo!

Moon Over Missouri

By DeWitt Scott

15

Cider Through A Straw

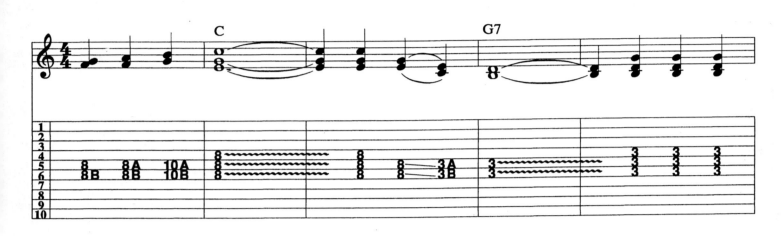

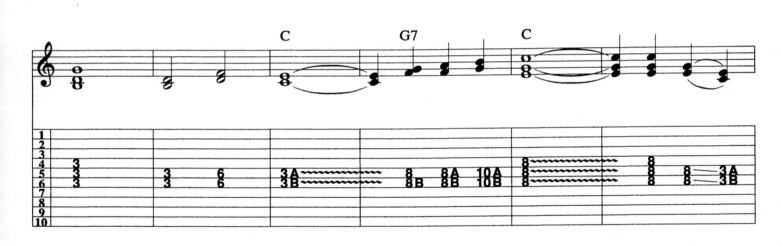

Cowboy Jack

I Never Will Marry

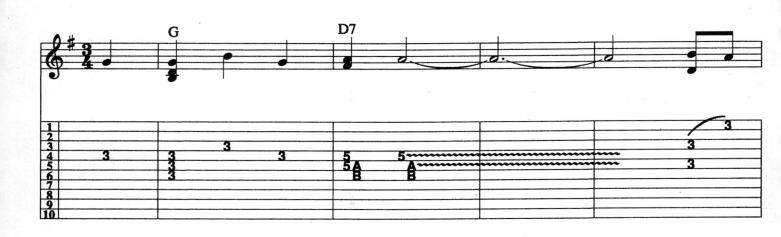

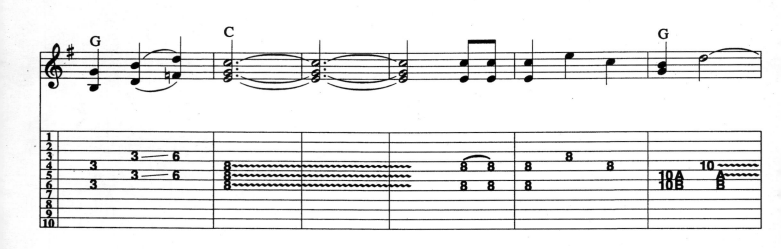

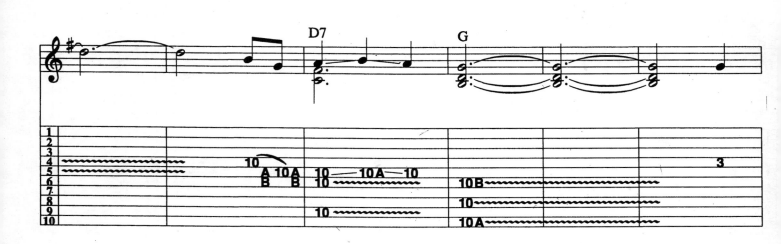

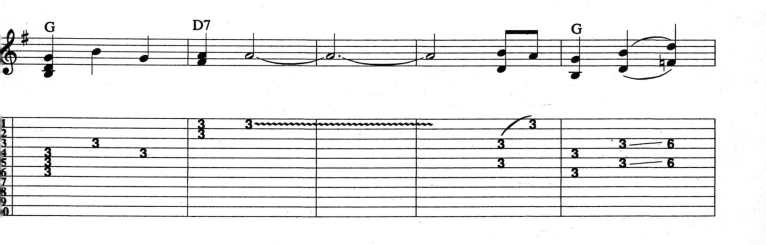

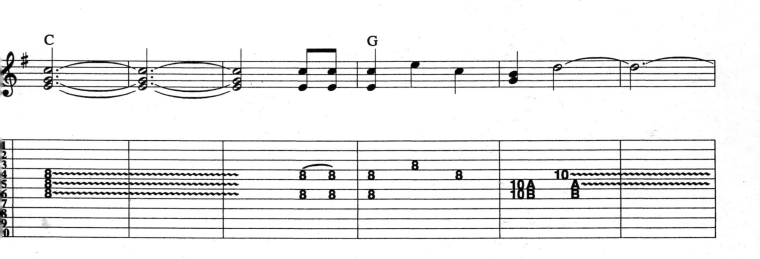

She'll Be Coming Round The Mountain

Amazing Grace

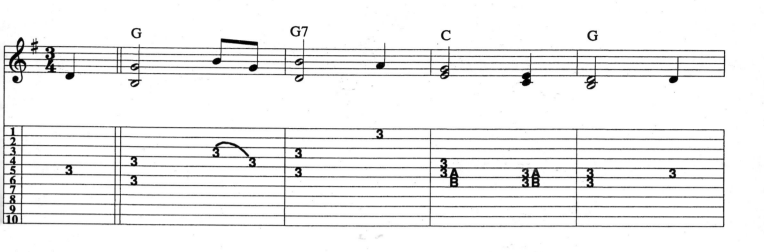

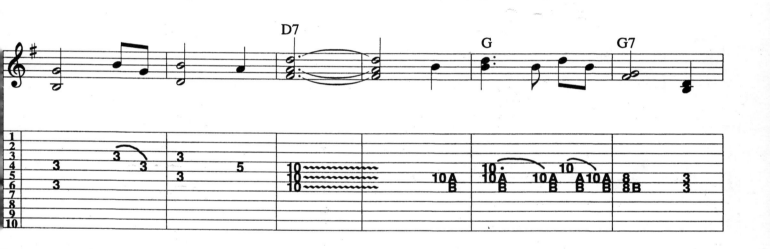

Will The Circle Be Unbroken

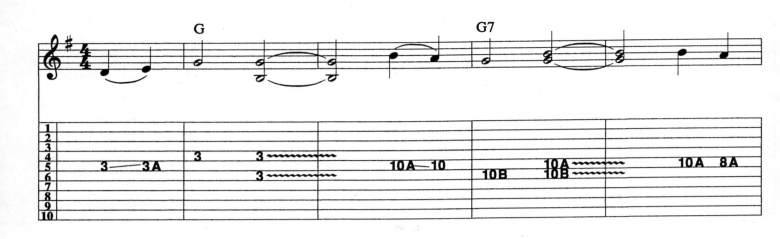

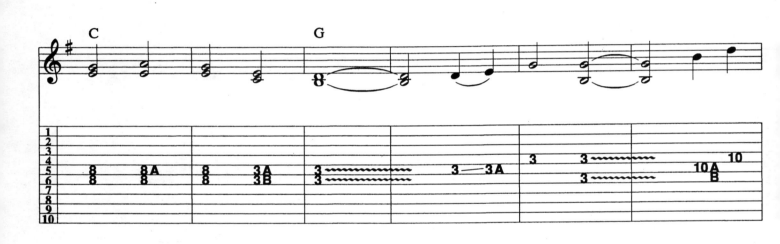

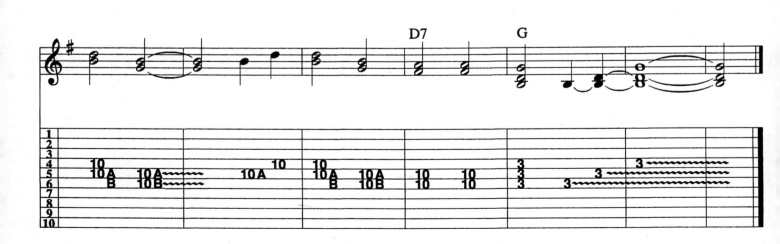

Down The Lonely Road

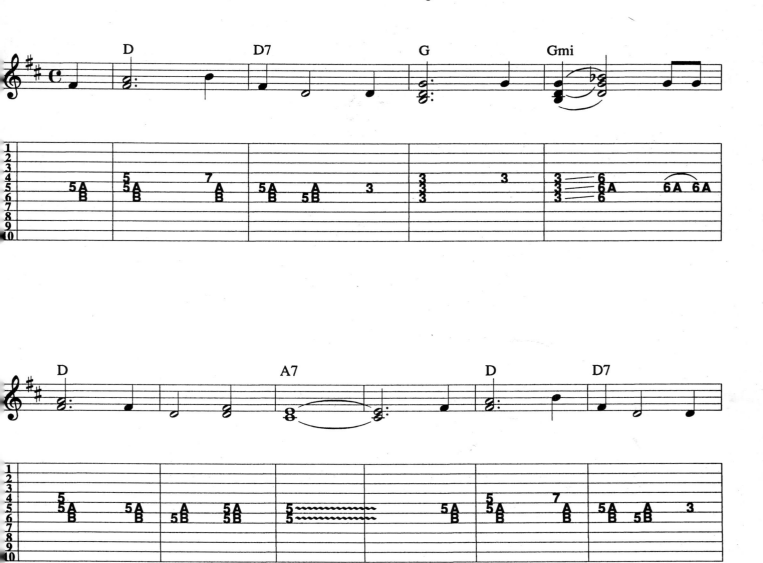

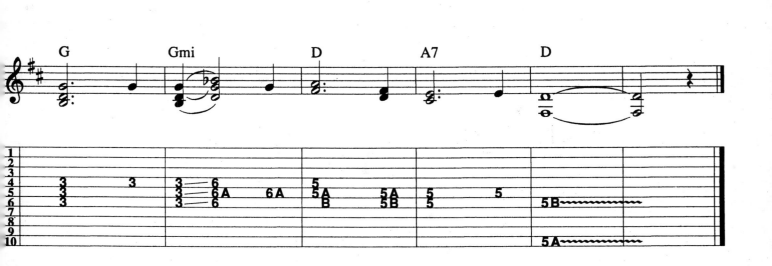

23

Just A Closer Walk With Thee

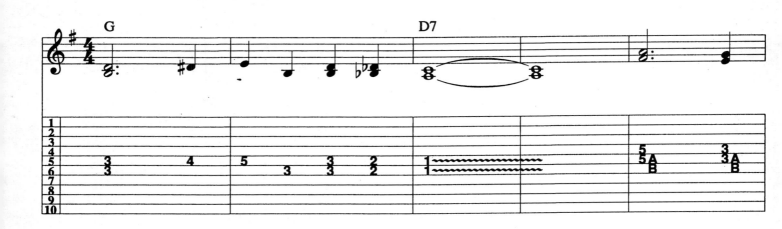

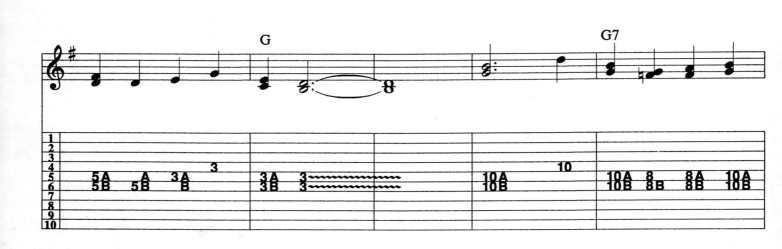

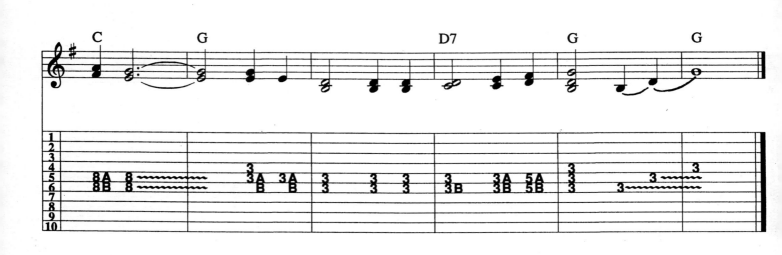

Aura Lee

Steel Guitar Waltz

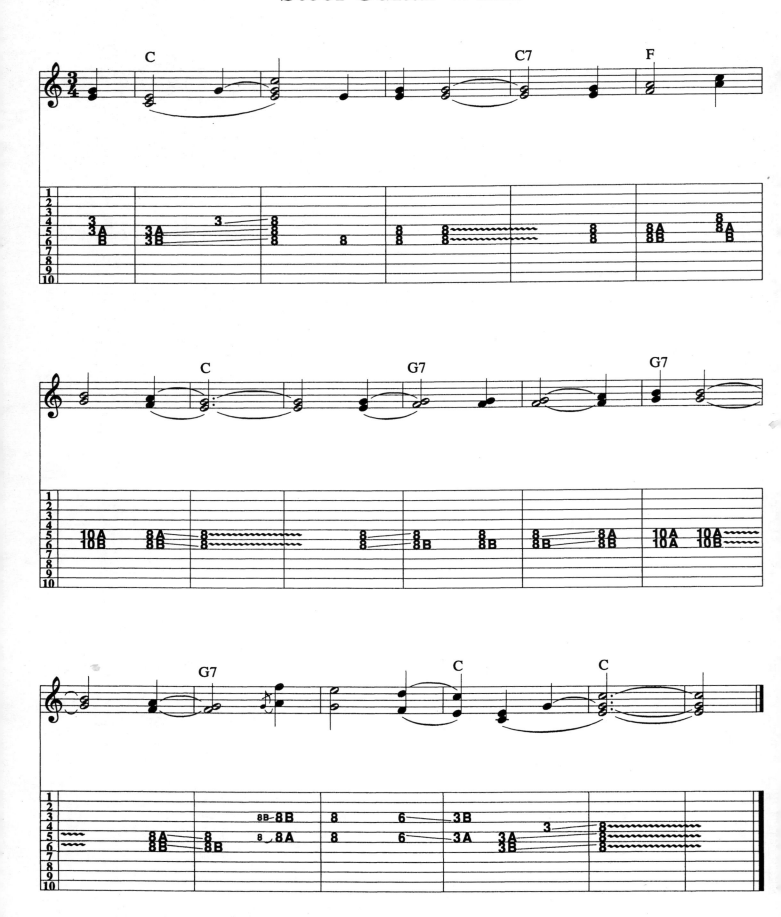

Pedal Steel Guitar Books and Videos

Mel Bay's Pedal Steel Guitar E9th Chord Chart
Mel Bay's Anthology of Pedal Steel E9th—Book and Cassette
Mel Bay's Deluxe Pedal Steel Guitar Method. E9th—Book and Cassette
Mel Bay's Back-Up Pedal Steel Guitar E9th—Book and Cassette
Tim McCasland Beginner Pedal Steel Guitar E9th—Video #1
Tim McCasland Beginner Pedal Steel Guitar E9th—Video #2
Lloyd Maines "Hot" Pedal Licks—Video

Non Pedal Steel Guitar Books

Complete Non Pedal Steel Guitar Method E7 Tuning—Book
The Art of Hawaiian Music—Book and Cassette

Dobro Books and Videos

Tim McCasland Beginner Dobro—Video
Tim McCasland "Famous" Dobro Solos—Video
Tim McCasland Dobro and Hot Licks Video
Learn to Play Bluegrass Dobro Guitar G Tuning Book
Dobro Songbook G Tuning—Book
Deluxe Dobro Tune Book G Tuning—Book and Cassette
Country Dobro Guitar Styles G Tuning—Book

Notes